The Magic of Love and Intimacy

Heart to Heart is Where We Start

by
Robert S. Cosmar

Du Bois PA

Magic Man's Universe Publishing
aka Barking Spiders Publishing

ISBN# 978-0-9839320-8-6

Awareness
Copyright 2011 Robert S. Cosmar

All Rights Reserved
First Printing -- 2011

Requests for information or interviews
should be addressed to:

> Robert S. Cosmar
> % Magic Man's Universe
> 705 W. Long Ave
> Du Bois, PA 15801
> 814-591-3363

Other Books by Robert S. Cosmar:
Trilogy of Awareness 2011
Awareness: Being Fully Alive

All rights reserved. No part of this publication may be reproduced, stored in a retrieval system or transmitted in any form or by any means -- electronic, mechanical, photocopy, recording or any other, except for brief quotations in printed reviews --without prior permission of the author, Robert S. Cosmar.

Printed in USA
Magic Man's Universe Publishing
aka Barking Spiders Publishing

Choices

Life is full of crossroads,
hard lefts and harder rights
with other paths and curves
going this way or that.
Each way has its own
set of bumps, and the
occasional hairpin turn.
Choices are new chances
to learn and grow
and gain more awareness.
We're never alone,
if we open our heart
our guidance whispers ...
Dusting myself off,
I've wondered at times
how my life might have
differed, had I taken
a different route.
Lord knows, I could have
used a few more straight
stretches along the way,
but at least I made choices,
some good, some not so good,
but each was perfect for me
at the time, creating
the being that now is.
How sad for those
who merely hitchhike
through life never daring
to choose at all.

by C.J. Heck

This book is dedicated to the love of my life,

Cathy Parrish (C.J. Heck),

whose support, dedication, encouragement and

editing have made all my works possible.

Introduction

Love is more than a word. It is the very fiber of existence. It is the glue that holds everything together and bonds everything on all planes of existence.

Intimacy is the ability to swim in the waves of love and allow love to reveal more of life's mystery and majesty.

Magic is what can happen when two hearts choose to bond through love, with intimacy and begin a journey of healing, revelation and creation.

When this happens we truly are Partners with the ever expanding Universe and ONE with all life and ourselves.

Sincerely,

Robert S. Cosmar

Table of Contents

The Dangers of the Cyber Confessional. 8

Enemies of Love 10

Anger in Relationships. 11

Almost, but not Quite!. 13

Passing the Torch of Love 15

The Girl with the Blue Eyes 18

The Gift of Love. 23

To Love a Woman 24

The Gift of Inner Healing. 26

The Nobility of the Feminine 28

So into You 30

What Good is Love if it does not Reveal More? 32

Partnership with the Universe 34

The Power of Devotion 36

Acceptance 38

Barriers to Intimacy 40

Being in Love 42

The Circle of Love 44

The Process of Pain in Love 46

The Path of Love 47

Discover the Meaning of Life though Partnership 49

The Intimacy of Caring 51

The Path of Love II. 53

The Magic of Courage in Intimacy 56

What is Love?? 59

The Dangers of the Cyber Confessional

The Internet has brought many wonderful opportunities to connect with others and share rewarding experiences. It has also allowed us to open our hearts and share our creations and unfortunately allowed us to sooth our egos at the expense of others. What people could not or would not deal with in the reality of their lives, they do dare to say or speak in the fantasy world of the internet. It is easy to say things nice and naughty to a person that you don't know or see, but is it real?

We all hear about people falling in love on the internet and the epidemic of cybersex, but what does this really say? Does it not say that in the area of our relationships and sexuality that something is wrong? In our day to day real lives we feel incapable of natural and real interaction. Our basic human needs for love and affection are not being met.

I am not saying that you cannot have a significant relationship online with someone in another part of the world or that you will not find someone to share your deepest fantasies with, but is it real? Are you able to have a deep interaction or intimacy that is healthy on all levels and not just candy for the ego? Yes, it is safe and you can say what you want, but what commitment are you making to yourself and another to grow in love and awareness? It is safe online, as long as you abide by societal laws, but even that can be blurred when you are vulnerable, needy and too curious. There is a dark side to the internet and a temptation to say what we want or feel without responsibility for the effect it has on others or yourself. It is much like being a kid that does something because they feel they will never be caught. Today you

have to be careful, because there are those watching in cyberspace for illicit or improper conduct, but a greater damage is done by us, to us when we choose to live our lives in a fantasy world, create fantasy relationships and do not deal directly with them in time and space. The damage is, that we merely create a false world to escape
the misery of the one we live in and we are still refusing to deal with ourselves and the person we are really.

Enemies of Love

Ego and mind are the enemies of love. They constantly compare, judge and seek to fill an imaginary void. Even when we're in love, they creep in and seek to dilute affection, intimacy and passion by taking unconscious experiences or pains and placing them into consciousness. These germs or viruses try and deceive us by concealing our true deep feelings of love. They betray what we know through our feelings and strive to make us identify with lies.

Every relationship, no matter how loving, has the challenges of these vices of mind and ego. Thoughts of doubt, jealousy, imagined hurts, perceptions tarnished through unconscious pain all corrupt feelings of love, because the mind is trying to gain control. Real love purifies perceptions, destroys illusions, and makes us unify our affections. Real love solidly grounds us in a relationship which is seeking fulfillment. You cannot love with all your heart, if your mind is cheating, lying, deceiving and betraying you or your lover. You cannot allow the love in your heart to migrates to the mind's arena.

It may not be a conscious intention, but unconscious and hidden by the ego, this is a resistance to surrender to love. Still there is fear that if you do, you will lose something of value, this value being the ego telling you that to surrender completely is to lose control. Control is the last hold the mind and ego have over you. Beyond that is Love and nothing more exists or prevents your completion into wholeness.

Anger in Relationships

Anger is rooted in a separation between mind and heart, and between our soul and our physical existence. Anger is a fear of losing control and facing nonexistence. It is a deep realization that we don't always have our way. It is a partner with surrender. A struggle always exists between the *me* and *you* in a relationship -- between me and my will and you and yours.

Harmony exists when both agree on what the other one wants, but often a subtle resentment lingers, when you realize you have to give in. The only resolution comes when you realize that everything happens for a purpose and, in the end, it does not matter who gets their way. Still, you sense inside the presence of your ego and it is wanting its way.

Relationships flow between moments of deep intimacy to periods of isolated distancing. Love at times functions like the tide. It comes in and it goes out, like a gentle ebbing and flowing of the heart. It never dies, but it has peaks and valleys of closeness and intimacy. There are periods when you feel closer to each other than other times.

Separation from each other physically or mentally can cause distress, because when you can't nurture the intimacy, all you have is a function of the mind called memory. Memories are not the real thing. They are mental energy living as imagination. This is why it is so hard to have a true and intimate long-distance relationship. Love needs intimacy, passion and physical closeness to grow and blossom. You can't have a true relationship over the phone or online.

It is normal at times to feel anger in a relationship. The happiness we feel in our hearts when it radiates with intimacy will soon flow to the mind as a memory and the ego will resent subtly that we gave in. The dynamics of love and the ego are very subtle, and so is anger. The mind and ego seek freedom for selfish purposes, while the heart only wants intimacy, harmony and cooperation. It is a challenge and a surprise at times to realize we have to juggle both anger and intimacy in a relationship. Not till we are whole, evolved and not needy can we rest from this struggle of our current condition of relating. The search for love in another still must to be found deep within ourselves first.

Almost, but not Quite!

Christmas is an opportunity to reconnect with loved ones and share a light-hearted time together, but it's also a sad time, because we never seem to really communicate even with our loved ones. Christmas has become so commercial and mostly an emotional roller coaster ride till it's over. Food becomes a substitute for a lack of nourishment that real intimate communication brings. We are all very sad and unfulfilled because we've not learned to open our hearts, or share and touch each other with the beauty within us. People spend their entire lives trying to be good at something rather than just being themselves. Instead of telling you who they are, they talk about what they do instead. This is not communion, it's reporting.

The human soul hungers for an intimacy of the heart that is shared deeply with others. Even our egos sense this need, but fear such vulnerability and hide with our deepest inadequacies. People are so afraid to be real and share their truths, always living in comparison with others and never feeling sufficient unto themselves. We do come closer at Christmas, but not close enough to embody the real spirit of this holiday. Maybe a hug is shared and an "I love you" said, but feelings deep inside are hidden or held back, even from those closest to us. How sad that we do not dare -- there is so much strength in sharing our vulnerability and intimate communion of the heart.

Words are symbols for ideas and when spoken without the heart, they're empty and hollow. Only when the passion of the heart enters do we feel the true spirit behind them. This is very healing and uplifting for all involved. So much of life is withheld and not fully lived when we don't realize what we feel and dare to share it honestly. We're all so caught up in artificial lives and uncertain how to be natural, loving and innocent in spirit. Gentleness is an attribute of an aware heart -- how much different Christmas would be if our hearts oozed gentleness during the Christmas season, but throughout the entire year, as well.

It's a sad truth I realized this past Christmas. You can know people for an entire lifetime, but never really communicate with them. They played a role for you, but your hearts never touched or revealed the sacredness within

Passing the Torch of Love

Love doesn't discriminate, judge or compare, only accepts all things unconditionally. Some of you may ask yourself how I feel about all this -- the journey Cathy is taking back into her past through her Memoirs From Nam blog, Vietnam, and the loss of Doug, her first real love. I'm going to tell you how I feel about it here in this blog. I hope for those of you who may be stuck in memories of past losses that you'll find hope, and realize that love never dies and it comes in many forms and many times.

When Cathy and I met again and we began to talk about our pasts, I knew her experience with losing Doug was a significant life experience and that her soul knew this as well. The deepest reasons for this I can't say, but I do know that when we have traumatic experiences, it's because our soul is trying to get us to look at unconscious patterns or things that prevent us from reuniting in awareness with different levels of ourselves. Most of us have our beliefs about the ultimate nature of existence and reality, but the truth is, we don't really know until awareness is brought through a shakeup of those beliefs.

When I asked Cathy to take me to Doug's grave, I knew it was the right thing to do. I don't know how I knew, but I did. My words poured honestly and sincerely from my heart as I talked to him there. I thanked Doug, after saying hello, and it felt like we were connected in some way. It felt like a cosmic channel between us had opened and we were talking in a meeting that seemed to have been prearranged in eternity past. It was a confirmation for me, that Cathy and I being together and the events around the reunion were all a part of a universal plan. I know she loves Doug and I'm sure, at times, she even wonders,

"What if". On that day, I *knew* Doug still loved her and I also *knew* I was now to carry that torch, the one of love between Doug and Cathy, after so many years of hollow promises in other relationships.

I am not jealous because I know I'm in a partnership with existence to help Cathy realize all the love inside her. Doug and I are pieces in the puzzle of her life and an integral part of the great mystery of existence. Neither of us own her, but we both are privileged to receive her trust and love to help us heal. It is never just about two people. Life involves all of us and we can never know who we've touched or who may be touching us, or when.

I made a promise to Doug that day to love her in the way he would have intended, with the same caring and feelings he felt for her. It was like a form of telepathic communicating where I could feel his energy and sense this was a high intent of his. I realize that I cannot prove any of this to those of you who read this, it's just something that you have to feel and experience in yourself. This was definitely not an everyday experience for us.

Love allows you to see the big picture of life and it goes well beyond the customs and beliefs of cultures and religions. What matters in life is what you feel about things. I feel that Doug, Vietnam and her loss of him is a part of the universe's plan for her growth in awareness. Her love is healing my issues and helping me to blossom more in my awareness.

Doug, wherever he may be now, realizes that the love he offered to her and shared with her was not in vain and it still continues through an agreement we three had together before this lifetime. Love is never about ownership, but an opportunity to experience greater awareness of both existence and spirit. Doug paid a price which I am sure has helped the three of us to become more aware of the nature of true reality and the deepest meaning of love -- a sacrifice for others.

I never knew Doug, because he was several years older than me. I do respect him. I respect what he did and how he touched my life and Cathy's and the three of us agree to do whatever it takes to help others to ascend in love and awareness towards the infinite mystery of life and existence

The Girl with the Blue Eyes

Life has its moments and images, some that stick with us forever. In the late 50's, I was going with my brothers and sisters to a local lake to swim and have some fun. Mom had arranged for us to pick up one of her high school best friends and her children to come along with us to the lake. I was sitting in the back of our station wagon when this girl with the most stunning blue eyes entered the car. I remember staring at her and her not looking at me at all. I was hypnotized by her eyes and unable to speak. At nine, I was too young, too shy, and too pre-hormonal to understand all that I was experiencing, but I think that was the first time I realized what a girl was and how the power of sexuality can slowly dawn on you.

That moment was never experienced again, as our families never went to the lake together again, as far as I can remember. I do remember many times hearing my parents talk about their friends and their children, but the girl with the blue eyes faded into my memories and somewhere into my unconscious sand over time that meeting was forgotten. I didn't remember her at all in high school, but she was two years older and we traveled in different circles. Yet to this day, I can vividly recall her in that back seat avoiding all eye contact with me.

Almost fifty years passed since I last saw her and, during that time, I had many lessons to learn and mistakes to make. She had her own journey of disappointments, despair and discovery to take. A couple of years ago, my sister was on her computer when she mentioned something to me about that same girl now being a children's author -- my sister was on her website now. I remember going over to look at the computer screen and seeing a picture of her. It brought back the memory of that day nearly fifty years earlier. She still had those stunning light-blue eyes and a soft sweet face. I got her email address and decided to comment on both her writing and the website and also share my interest in astrology and spirituality. I was curious to see what she might have to say. A day or so after that, I received my answer. It was not as glorious as I had hoped. She was going through a divorce at the time and her response seemed rather cold and distant. I accepted that, forgot about the email response, and went on living my life

Somewhere in 2008, after talking to an old high school friend, I made the decision to organize a multi-class high school reunion. It was one of those things I felt compelled to do and didn't exactly know why, especially since I had to do most of the work alone or with very little help. Still, I was determined to see it through, because I felt deep inside that it was important to me and to many others. Again, I didn't know why. It was as though I sensed a promise that If I stayed the course, something wonderful was going to happen.

Over the next two years, I organized, talked to people, and found myself writing emails of a very personal and spiritual nature. Somehow I knew I had to be true to myself, my feelings, and the vision that had unfolded within me for the reunion. I began to write from my heart and to trust the whispers, knowing that some would be offended, but also realizing there were others who felt the same way but were unable to express those feelings as easily.

One day while I was at work, I got a surprising email from the girl with the blue eyes. She hadn't heard about the reunion and one of her classmates had forwarded my emails to her. Those whispers from my heart to others had touched hers and opened her to me. She told me how much the words meant to her and it was almost like she was saying, "Here I am, I'm ready now. Where do we go from here?" Playfully, I teased her about her blue eyes and shared how I remembered them 50 years earlier. It was all very natural, heartfelt and it seemed so right. Something was happening.

Over the next few months before the reunion, she and I shared emails and stories. Romance and a relationship were not even spoken of at the beginning. We just sensed we had to follow the friendship and the feelings to see if they would eventually end ... or something else might take its place. As time went on, I found myself having the courage to be more open and honest with her and more revealing of my past. She was uneasy with some of my past and, at one point, we both even felt the urge to walk away, but something would not let us.

One night at home. I was laying on my back in the grass under the stars in my yard talking to her on the phone. I told her about my deepest heartbreak in love. It was the first time I had ever opened my heart and it had been rejected. That night under the stars, I was sure she and I had come to the end of the line. As I had it analyzed up to this point, we didn't have a whole lot in common, or so it seemed. But when I was done telling her about the pain I had carried around of that past love, she said something that touched me deeply. She said : "I would never hurt you like that." It seemed to be more than words, it was like a promise and I knew she would keep it. That was the door I needed, the door that took me beyond my fears and handed me the encouragement to continue trusting her.

For the first few months, as we were getting to know one another, she would not allow me to call. She was hesitant to hear my voice. She wouldn't allow me to visit, because she was hesitant to see me. It was so frustrating to be held at bay, because I wanted and needed to talk to her, be with her. I knew in my heart she loved me.

Later, just before we first met, she tortured me with things like, "Robert, if it's love, it will be in the eyes. When you love someone, they will see it in your eyes." She also told me she wouldn't know for sure that it was love until she could smell the little place at the nape of my neck. The nose knows ... seems I had to pass this test before she would really know if we were right for each other. I was unsure of why she needed this but I was trusting my heart and our feelings.

We met for the first time in person the night before the reunion at a little inn in the town where she and I were raised. She opened the door and, for the first time in almost 50 years, I saw those blue eyes again and a smile to boot. While we hugged, she buried her face in my neck. It was a warm, sweet and endearing embrace. It felt natural and right without either of us saying a word. I knew I loved her and I also knew she loved me.

An air of intimacy seemed to envelop us and no matter where we went, we felt compelled to be touching, whether sitting close together, or holding hands and staring silently into each other's eyes and getting lost there. It felt then, and still does, like we're hooked deeper than our minds, emotions and even bodies. Our journey to love had been long, sometimes painful and confusing. Over the years, I had given up my search for the right girl and, in a way, she no longer searched for mister right. We had arrived at a time in our lives when we stopped hoping and looking ... and then this something magical happened. The mystery of love brought us together so we could experience more of life together and learn together what it means to be in love for real.

.... and you know what ? She was right. I saw the love in her eyes and when I breathed her in, her scent went all the way to my soul.

The Gift of Love

What is this mysterious thing we call love? Why do we desire it? What compels us to find it and want to explore it? Most feel it is for procreation and emotional happiness, but it actually has a much higher purpose. Love is a feeling that reveals a connection beyond our own small *self*. It is a unifying link to something well beyond the mind and our eyes to sense and see. Love reveals our deeper and truer nature and it also is the master key to truth and an understanding of life.

To be in love, you must sacrifice the need to be in control and have your way all the time. It is the surrender of the ego to serve another's needs and wants. It is opening your heart to give without the fear of being taken advantage of. A person who serves another with the intention of *getting* is not in love. That type of love is conditional and so limited. Lovers give for the sheer joy of feeling a completeness within themselves. They realize that to live in the heart is to be in harmony with each other and all of existence.

Love is not static, but is dynamic and changeable. You can't imprison or copy a loving moment, nor can you duplicate or hide it under a bushel basket. It reveals *everything* to us and it also exposes us to ourselves and others. It will never be denied and you can't avoid it. Love is a mystery, because it comes from the mystery of who we are. All the treasures of existence are revealed in Love. It is the one thing you can seek and never find. Love also cannot be bought, because it is a gift from existence to you ... for when you are ready.

To Love a Woman

To love a woman is not a simple matter, but then it is. For her, her heart is open and wanting to receive the love inside you. For most men this is a slow and scary proposition. Men are taught from birth that the world is a place of conflict, competition and all of the rewards are based on effort alone. Money is required to make it out there, or you will suffer humiliation and loss of respect. Men are forced from birth to close down, buckle up and bear the burden of struggle.

Most women, on the other hand, are brought up to nurture others, to care for people and to simply *feel*. She cries easily, feels hurt when she witnesses wrong and learns to bury her disappointment emotionally when her natural healing love is pushed away. For a lot of women, the promise of love is cut short by men too afraid to lay down their imaginary fears. The power of love's attraction can and does bring two people together, but it does not guarantee completion. Only a lazy person can think that attraction brings lasting love -- it does not.

Women are committed to love mostly. Men slowly and fearfully approach it as if it is a poison of some sort. Women understand human nature and realize men are afraid and need patience, but men are at times too afraid to tell the truth within themselves and hide the realities of what years of feeding their pride and ego have done to them. How shut down, alone and fearful they are.

Women spend way too much time and effort trying to rehabilitate a man. Some are abused verbally, physically and emotionally. Men who cannot surrender their fears to a woman cannot grow or heal. They have been told all along what a man is *supposed* to be, but they never learned how to feel, cry or be just a real person without the guilt.

Men suffer from an identity crisis of what a man actually is. In love, many are not fully surrendered or trusting enough to grow beyond the physical or emotional attraction. They stop discovering themselves within the honesty of love and the woman they love withers on the vine. Women need affection, caring and a need to feel that they are loved. Daily they need to feel that love, not only hearing in words but through feelings and within their lover's actions. There is an energy to love, and love is not just a word. It is this energy that is the cement of love. Some of it is transmitted through loving sex between partners, most of the time it is felt in a kiss, a hug or cuddling on a couch. Spooning in bed is another form of sharing this natural affection. It is a healing seal of love.

A man must conquer the self he has been made into to love a woman. She waits for his tears, his fears and his failures to help heal the wounded heart he carries inside. She can and often is a source of strength when he falls or stumbles. The greatest mistake a man in love makes is when he fails to trust and love her fully; fails to surrender each fear, every doubt and all barriers within him to her naturally nurturing soul. Allow love to reveal its depth and strength in a lasting bond and commitment to each other. This is the promise of love, but not a guarantee of it. Time is needed and choices have to be made to reveal if the fruit of real love is ripe on the tree of life. This I know to be true because my mate and love have shown me it is so.

The Gift of Inner Healing

It is one thing to fall in love, another to be in love and still another to stay in love. Love grows and deepens if we allow it. It blossoms like a flower and leaves a fragrance to smell in your heart and feelings. Love shares everything and hides nothing. It reveals all the blemishes and seeks to heal them. It keeps you vulnerable and naked and warm inside. It flows between two people and reveals the deep communion shared by all existence.

To be in love is to be alive to everything and each other with a sensitivity that is light and healing. I am often amazed at those moments of realization between me and Cathy at how deep and far reaching the love is between us. I never thought love could be this good or reveal this much.

Love to me was a thing. Something that you need to find and get. Not something that you need to already have and want to share. I was like most people or more specifically most men that feel that love owes them or that life owes them. Life does not owe us anything. It already gave us the gift of life and the freedom to discover what that means. We have to discover, explore and give all that we are if we are to know love and search its depth. We have to let go of the fear and the small "I" to realize a communion with the "AM" of existence. It is no coincidence that we feel better when we give of ourselves to others. Those selfless moments open the heart and connect us with others. The depth of that connection depends on the level of intimacy and vulnerability present.

Vulnerability may be a sign to the mind and ego of unworthiness, but to the heart it is a door to inner healing and surrender to those parts of you most able to renew and heal you. Inner healing is called inner healing because it is inner. Outer healing is a byproduct of the power of the inner to heal the body and mind, but true inner healing puts us back in wholeness with life. It fills the gap that the mind creates and completes the circle of existence. Today is Cathy's birthday and I wanted to surprise her and honor her for coming into my life and becoming such a gift of inner healing to me.

The Nobility of the Feminine

It is natural for the female to give, to surrender and to feel. By their very nature they are closer in essence to the universe.

This is something they sense biologically, spiritually and psychologically. It is for this reason that they live longer than men do. Men seek to control, dominate and compete -- it is for this reason that they are further from the nature of the universe. Something in man fears, and fears deeply. Man feels that he must prove himself, but a woman just tries to be herself.

The receptivity in a woman that allows her to trust herself is what gives her power over men. Men seek refuge and rest in women, a place to hide from life's brutality -- a brutality they have created. Her knowing is her mystery, and that is why men are baffled and amazed. She can do more in less time than many men can achieve simply because she is more adapted to working together with others. She nurtures and brings people together. She understands harmony and cooperation. From the heart, she commands the excellence of her being.

By her very presence, a man is subtly drawn in and he feels the pull of her gravity upon him. She can silently massage his heart and help him to awaken to himself. She can make a man feel like a king and, she can take away his crown in a moment, such is the power of the feminine. You may want to argue with her, but be prepared to be defeated, because in her knowing, she has already held your heart in her hands. She knows where she is going and you don't.

Not all women possess this grace of their being, but many do, and this is what gives sense to civilization and why all women are the mothers of cooperation. They know that to survive, you must meet others halfway. You must be willing to see deeper than your side of things, and know that life is not a race, but a flowering, if it is lived within the heart and allowed to blossom naturally. You can try to beat her down but in the end, she will win, because she knows she has a heart and she knows how life is best lived.

So Into You

Have you ever heard someone say that they were so *into someone*, such as a lover? I used to wonder about that, until I fell in love for the first time at 58. I had many relationships over the years, but none reached the depth or intimacy until Cathy came into my life. It was more than just mind and emotion. It was like a melting into, or maybe a mending of, something. It was like something that had been missing was activated and a warm flow of intimacy took over and bonded us together.

I have felt all along that love was a dynamic thing and not a static. It just does not appear, and that is it. Love is dynamic, revealing, healing, and awakens you to feelings that you were not privy to before. It makes you conscious of a need to keep the love flowing and that love can and will guide you to deeper levels of experience within it. It promotes a will to harmony and unselfishness. You become partners in love and the social convention of marriage did not create this.

Marriage, for some people, can be poison to their love. It is taking a real feeling and putting too many expectations and restraints on it. It is saying to the mind this is how to preserve the love and how to make the marriage last, when the very act of marriage never had anything to do with love in the first place. Marriage does not make you love someone more. It can prevent you from knowing them and learning from the feeling of love that drew you together. Love is not an institution. It is the process through which awareness reveals the nature of the universe and ourselves to us. Love is the opposite of division -- marriage, by labeling love, divides it.

In my relationship with Cathy, I have felt a common destiny guiding us and an awareness of the importance of growing further into love, by letting love reveal and guide all the parts of our lives -- allowing it to help us to discover who we are, what we do, and how and when to do it. Love simply reveals that you know, but do you trust what you know? I have found that when you fail to allow the love to guide you as a couple, it can create awkward, clumsy and hurtful experiences. Love can die between two people, but only when walls of self protection are built up and true communication from the heart breaks down, or even ceases.

It is not just to bring two people together that love exists. Love both includes individuals and transcends them. It can reveal the mystery of why people feel so *into* each other in love, or it can be a doorway into the universe and how it operates. A third element exists in a relationship of love. It is what bonds two people together and also what guides them forward to discover more about themselves and life. Love makes us see things through our hearts and shows us why love is the essence of existence.

What good is Love if it does not reveal more?

Is this *it*? Have you ever found yourself in a relationship and asked yourself that question? People seem to feel that, after marriage, their relationship has reached a peak and that it will just automatically go into the future blissfully. They then are shocked and dismayed to realize that elements of resistance exist in the relationship that must be dealt with. You begin to learn what a committed relationship really is and what it takes to keep it going. Some people go through an entire marriage or relationship and never grow in their awareness of each other. They go through the motions, play the game, and yet remain hidden from each other.

In love, you cannot hide. If you want love to grow and live between you both, it has to live in your hearts and feelings. This can only happen when you remain open to each other and openly share what you are experiencing. When you are in a love relationship, each of you have brought with you a whole lifetime of your own experiences, pain, hurts, and issues that need to be shared and experienced in an atmosphere of love and acceptance. In a real love relationship, you encourage your lover to reveal themselves in an atmosphere of acceptance and love. It is necessary for both parties to accept and heal and then let go, those things which stood in the way of loving in the past.

It is hard for people to share their faults and fears with each other. It's very personal to reveal the darkness we all have inside. But it is absolutely necessary, if we are to grow in awareness of love and within ourselves. When you hide the truth about yourself from another, you keep a block, a wall, in between you and them -- a block in the flow of love that is already there and waiting to reveal something even deeper and more fulfilling to both of you. This is why vulnerability is so important. Compassion is kindred to love and a helping hand to a wounded soul.

No one can know the power of love to heal if they don't risk a total revealing of self to a lover. It is not a onetime thing, but a continual process of honesty from the soul, a truth that reveals a depth of consciousness shared and extended on into eternity. We are all partners with the universe, unfortunately, we don't all accept the invitations, the very gifts, that love offers us.

Partnership with the Universe

Do you hear it? Can you feel it? Have you experienced it? Something is happening and it is affecting our relationships. People are waking up to their feelings and putting aside the values and opinions of the past in their relationships. No longer do people just want sex, companionship or marriage, THEY WANT LOVE and something so much more.

We are at a time in the evolution of things where people are earnestly seeking and finding love. This is most likely not something they chose, but something which they stumbled upon accidentally. Maybe they gave up looking or got out of a bad relationship, but then it happened. Someone popped in unexpectedly and feelings began to speak to them with no logic or rationale, just gut feelings, both deep and silent, calling each to an intimacy with each other and something more.

While sex is an intimacy of bodies, love is an intimacy of souls. You can have physical sex that will satisfy somewhat the body and emotions, but without love, it goes no deeper and cannot touch and massage the hearts. It will not give the feeling of an inseparable bond, a partnership, of consciousness. Lovers are called to share more than bodies and emotions. They are called to join in a oneness of consciousness that reaches deeper than this world and lands into the next. Love is the invitation to taste and share one-ness, to create together from the well of life.

You cannot find love, it finds you, at least the real love does. The real love and the word love have nothing in common. The real love knows itself, no questions need to be asked, the false love or the idea of love has many suspect variations based in emotion and thought and sensual pleasure. It does not go deep enough to be real, it only speaks to desires unfulfilled and not the hearts yearning for nourishment. Real love is always looking to give and share with another, the false is always wondering what it can take from the other. No one is ever fully satisfied with the false love.

You may be yearning to have a relationship, to love and be loved, dreaming of deep sensual passion and lust within yourself, but ask yourself this question? WHAT DO YOU HAVE TO GIVE TO ANOTHER TO AWAKEN THEIR HEART? You can't buy love as the song goes, but some people think so, and spend a lifetime bribing others to love them. It will not work. You have to have something precious, something learned through failure and pain, a humbleness, a vulnerability an openness to be loved.

The Power of Devotion

After trust, intimacy, and cooperation, comes devotion. Devotion is a recognition that you have found a level of deep harmony in a relationship. Hearts have opened and embraced and the mind no longer wanders. You feel a connection to each other and something more. It is this something more that gives the magic feel to a relationship. It is the purpose for why two lovers meet and a potential indicator of what the relationship can achieve in partnership with the universe.

Relationships are a doorway for people to achieve higher awareness of themselves and life, if they have been brought together in love. Devotion is a level of growth in a relationship of love where unconscious beliefs and habits dissolve and a clarity of unity begins to unfold between two people. They think and feel alike. Creatively, they are able to dance with the universe playfully and bring forth inspirations from their hearts to enjoy and share with others. They have found a home in their hearts together and they sit on the steps of the universe and wonder what's next.

The power to create and enjoy a blissful relationship with life is based on this principle of devotion. A scattered or disturbed mind has little power to achieve. Two minds in mutual conflict live in hell, but two surrendered hearts achieve a cooperation with life and the universe and are granted the privilege of co-creating a future that heals and allows two people to experience the fullest measure of their potentials together. Your intimacy together blends with the intimacy of life.

You remember who and what you are together and you understand the mysteries of life effortlessly, because the mind is no longer in conflict with existence. You experience truth as an extension of your being and not a theory to be followed or idealized. There is nothing sweeter than to remember together and share these memories in a new awareness. Two have become ONE and oneness is the true nature of all existence.

Most people will surrender their bodies in a relationship for sex; some will share their minds and emotions, but few will surrender to the heart of each other and build trust, which leads to intimacy for cooperation in a purpose that can only manifest in devotion. To work with life and the universe, you have to achieve a devotion to each other and a devotion to the purpose of your partnership with the universe.

When unity is found at the core of apparent division, an explosion of purpose bursts forth and clarity is achieved to manifest a vision that is buried deep in the hearts of all lovers. The gift of shared love is that you are joined to the universe in a playful dance of possible outcomes. Nothing is set in stone, but as a couple, you are given the freedom to explore and learn the meaning of existence and your places in it forever.

Acceptance

When we are not born into complete acceptance we are unable to bring through the love we felt in the other world, the universe. This love or awareness is a recognition of our full self. Because of the fear of our parents and society and the deep distrust of self and life, a gap begins between who we were and now who we are asked to be.

Great demands are placed on a child to conform and behave according to the views of society and our parents. Doctors, teachers and ministers all unwittingly conspire to make the child distrust and forget the innocence from which they came, forgetting the invisible friends and voices that children often hear. Children are shut down and taught to fear, just like the grownups do. This fear and distrust carries over into all other relationships. In school and dating, great fear and ignorance is forced onto the consciousness of children.

Rather than being told to trust and believe in their feelings, many have formed judgments and suspicions that have no base in reality. This does not mean dangers do not exist, but the individual freedom to decide in each experience is blinded by group paranoia.

If people are truly sick mentally and spiritually it is not because their inherent nature is bad before birth, but rather because many of the idea's of humanity are restrictive, oppressive and malignant and they are polluted after birth. A child is only able to bring through at birth that essence which the parents are able to receive and nourish. If the parents do not know love, acceptance and have awareness, then the child's magic is polluted.

Children are born magically innocent with the power to touch a heart, but their ability to create is years away and to understand the voices they heard as a child. If they can remember, they can put together a whole life of happiness, if not then they will struggle in the maze of false perceptions that exist with us here on earth.

To be truly happy you must learn to accept everything, both the apparent good and bad. You must come to acknowledge that life is a mirror for your beliefs. Forgive your parents and society for their limited perceptions and begin to heed the whispers of your deep inner self and follow the sounds of your own soul. Life is not against you, but at birth you were forced to not accept the total reality of who and what you are, what you can do and become and why you are here..

Barriers to Intimacy

I have heard people say that you have to accept the issues of another person if you are to have a relationship with them. I agree somewhat with this, but if you accept the issues and do not explore their roots, you cannot continue to grow in the awareness of love. Love is not static, it is dynamic and multifaceted. It breaks down the walls of division and reveals a underlying unity in all things and between them. You cannot grow in love if you avoid issues or hide behind them

Love forces you to examine yourself and to bare your heart and soul to a lover at times. It can be risky and fearful, but when you are in love, you are NEVER closer to another human being, never more vulnerable and trusting. It must be a full disclosure of fears, doubts and failings, but this is buoyed by hope, acceptance and a realization that something precious is to be gained by confronting the issues within ourselves, sharing them, and then putting them behind us. Wholeness, synergy and a triangle of creativity is the prize two lovers strive towards and can attain. You can create your destiny together in a partnership with your very existence, "God" or the universe. You become aware of the real nature of things and of yourselves as conscious eternal beings

You cannot be in love and hold onto past issues. Something deep inside echoes that a stillness and peace within are to be attained, but only if you dare to jointly confront and discard the barriers to true growth in love and intimacy. It is for this reason that lovers meet somewhere in the middle to confront and dissolve the issues and walls that exist in their own unconscious minds. Each is a mirror for the other to look into their deepest self while being comforted in the arms of their lover.

For a relationship to flourish, there black must be intimacy. It takes a lot of courage to say to your lover, "Hey, this is me. I'm not proud of it -- in fact, I'm embarrassed by it -- but this is the real me. This is who I am."

Being in Love

... for most people, is easier said than done. I try in my blog to be honest and insightful about things and I share my heart with my readers. At times, being in love is a challenge -- to be in love and reap the benefits of loving another person can feel as if you are one inch from slipping into hell or an abyss. It is so easy to blame the other person for our pain and grief. We do not want to admit it is our fault and that we have to change our way of relating. We tend to avoid our responsibility at all costs for our own failure to grow in a relationship.

Trusting another person is a risk that we do not easily accept. Hell, we barely trust ourselves, or God, or the Universe itself. Life at times seems like a cross between hell and madness with periods of blissful happiness. We are not sure yet what life is all about and even who we are. We use the word love loosely and we are putting the cart before the horse. We don't know love -- we are seeking to find it, or understand it and not lose it.

When it comes to another person we have to be vulnerable to discover trust. We have to risk revealing all the gory details of who we are and share them at the appropriate time. It will seem at times that things come up that you dread or fear to share and it is precisely those things that stand in the way of a deepening love. If you are really in love, a force inside you has called you to be with a person to learn about yourself, to heal the split we all have inside us. It is an opportunity to complete your journey of awareness in partnership and to learn your depths of joy and sorrow cradled at times in the arms of a lover. It is a wonderful joy, being in love with another person and, as each experience attests, a sense of expectation of fulfillment grows with each challenge as it is faced. Your mind can't explain it, but your hearts know that you are following a path in uncharted territory to discover something about yourself and each other. People who do not know love struggle and fight and abuse each other constantly. Their minds yearn for a mystery that their hearts can only know. They are not ready to surrender because they believe falsely that they already know the answers. No one knows the answers, there are none. Life simply *is* and it reveals itself when you take the risk to love.

The Circle of Love

When I have looked at all the successful relationships I have had, my friendships and my relationship with Cathy, these three words are at the essence of them **Trust, Respect, and Cooperation**. It does not matter if you are in a love relationship, a friendship or a business partnership. These three words are MAGIC. They build on each other, complement each other and drive each other into a lively interplay of energy that is creative, joyful and fun.

Trust is the beginning of any relationship. With it comes a faith that no matter how hard the times get, you will still succeed because something deep inside you compels you to see it through. Something says it will be worth it all. Still, to trust is to be vulnerable and with it, the possibility to be hurt. It is to risk abandonment and misunderstanding. It exposes your innocence, ignorance and gullibility. It tests you to see if you know and believe that everything happens for a purpose and reason and that the universe is always supporting a greater growth in awareness and love.

Respect follows on the heels of trust. It is seeing into the goodness of each other and it brings a deeper awareness that life has a plan and a purpose. You begin to work together and create together and bring out the very best in each other. You become aware of an inter-connectivity between each other and a synergy exists that is directed to a common objective. You begin to accept yourself more easily and believe in those talents and gifts you once thought were oddities. You find that you want to express yourself more earnestly and share those secret gifts and talents that you once thought meant nothing.

Nothing gets achieved without cooperation. It is a selfless surrender to help another achieve a goal or plan without having to control or demand that everything has to be your way. People who trust and respect each other are in ONE agreement. They work in harmony and achieve because they help each other and feel the needs of the other are in some ways more important than theirs. They see that to help the other is to help themselves in the long run. It becomes a cycle of giving that spirals upward, lifting the spirits of both and allowing time for other things to be done. Cooperation feeds trust, trust feeds respect and respect leads to greater cooperation. It is a giant circle whose innermost essence is that word we call love.

The only things in life that are worth doing are those things we do for the common good of all.

The Process of Pain in Love

Love is a roller coaster of pain and pleasure. Sometimes we feel pleasure and security in it and at other times fear and all kinds of insecurities. It is all normal and provides us with the possibility to grow in understanding and awareness. When you fight and have disagreements you are addressing buried fears and issues that prevent or block true intimacy. It is necessary to go thru these experiences so you can discover the reason why love has not blossomed in your life.

Lovers feel close and intimate with each other. Not just while making love, but a good part of the time in general. They don't like being separated, because the mind tricks the heart from feeling the connection that love brings. You feel a magic and a great sensitivity to life when you are in love, a connection to something beyond the relationship. That connection is the purpose of love. Lovers do fight and argue and feel hurt, but real lovers seldom abuse each other. Abuse is the result of fears that are triggered within and not handled responsibly by both parties.

If your relationship is not HOT at times then it lacks an opportunity to blossom and grow. It will also lack passion and compassion as you will not be addressing the issues within that need healed. You will have entered a relationship with thick hard walls and barriers to true intimacy. It is no fun to be in a one way relationship, to give and give and never get. Martyr's are not good companions and control freaks never learn to share the fear and pain they need to release.

The Path of Love

The Path of Love leads towards unity. Whenever we are loved we feel complete, peaceful and whole. Something in us becomes alive that is usually hidden by thought, emotion and desire. We simply know that all is well and we are safe. No dread exists and the pain inside us is diminished. Life is blissful when we are loved and the future appears bright and hopeful.

The interesting thing about love is that you can't find a simple description for it or a quick answer. No two people experience love the same way or see it alike, still, when we feel it, it gives the same result. Like life, love is a multidimensional experience and seems to be tailored to each person through their own specific experiences, persons and events. At first, we do not seem to appreciate events as being loving, that make us feel vulnerable and scared, but in time all events reveal a hidden mystery behind them that is meant for us only.

Strangely love can't be learned. Some people may disagree with me, but mimicking a loving act is not loving in reality. You can try to teach a child to be loving by not hitting another child, but inside you can't make them love another child. Love must be discovered by feeling the result of hate and pain. Life is a continuum of extremes or opposites where we need to see each side of an event to know it totally. You cannot feel the height of joy unless you have experienced deep pain and sorrow.

In this life we are taught to see certain experiences as positive and desired and others as negative and undesired. For this reason, many people never reach a full understanding in themselves of the truth of where they are.

They seek to avoid the gift in a painful experience and never learn why it repeats itself over and over in their life. They are divided in their understanding and can't unify or harmonize the painful experience into positive growth. Life has both good and bad experiences by label or definition. They both lead to the same realization: which is, we are connected to our experiences in many, and deep, ways and our world perspective is molded by them. Our world is as we are inside at all times.

Love deepens awareness. It allows us to see and feel the best in us. It shows us that good things can happen when we are coming from a deep connectedness inside us. Nothing is ever wasted in existence. No event is useless or without cause. You learn to be aware from the painful results of embracing illusions. The Path of love is to awaken in you a personal connection to the vastness of existence and your own special place within it. Never fear a defeat, a heartache or a loss. The pain is dissolving the illusion so that you can see the light, or reality, of truth. Only by seeing the truth can you build a future that is loving and supportive of all that is around you..

Discover the Meaning of Life through Partnership

Great awareness can come out of relationships, if both parties are unafraid to reveal their true self to each other, and if they see the relationship as a tool to understanding their inner workings, beliefs and complexes.

Too often, people seek a relationship to calm their emotional storms and sexual urges. These relationships often end on the rocks because the connection is superficial and not deep and lasting. People walk away angry, frustrated and blaming each other for the failure to make it last. They do not see that each of them is triggering pain deep inside the other and, while it seems to be the other person's fault, it is still THEIR pain. It comes from inside you and it is a key as to why you feel cut off from life.

Till death do you part is only realized by people lucky enough to have found love. Love calls you to unity, it reveals hopes and it also binds you to discover those fears, doubts and illusions that prevent you from being more conscious and aware. It is for your Being and not just your body. Love is an energy that permeates everything, but it is separated from us by the duality of existence. *Mind* is the opposite of *being*. Thought is a bridge for being to relate to mind in our outer reality. A barrier exists between being and thought and that is mind. It allows us to function in this realm as a separate ego, still connected to being but unaware of its location or presence. Our aloneness is our lack of awareness of our totality as beings.

Partnership in love is an opportunity to weaken the ego and bridge the consciousness through the heart to the soul. It allows for awareness to blossom and healing of the unconscious. It helps to show us that life can be easier when we come from a level of deep awareness and magic does exist. Life can be a dance and a synergy with the divine. Our power is revealed through partnership as we realize that we become conscious of a cooperation that exists with the greater parts of our beings. Together, we share in its vision and revelation. We are tools for the divine to reveal its nature, purpose and truth.

So little respect today exists for love, partnership and marriage. The sacredness has been forgotten. The energy is misunderstood and the purpose polluted. Still, it lingers and waits for the mystery of love to breathe on two souls and say come hither, come together, come as the whispers beacon you deeper beyond the strife to the clarity of being and existence.

The Intimacy of Caring

If there is one thing that separates lovers from other relationships it would be a feeling of deep caring and intimacy. Lovers feel a connection deep within, much more than physical, and far deeper than emotional. It is as though the two have become one person. Your awareness becomes two-person centered and no longer self-centered. You sincerely care for the other and their well being. You give of yourself to lighten the burden of their life. You support their efforts without judgment or criticism. You become their mirror of inspiration and a deep well of comfort and compassion. You both come to understand the power of harmony and balance, the deep power of oneness at the core of your existence. You realize that deep caring and intimacy are a healing for the pain you felt in your alone years. What this is, is a connection to something beyond your "I" and it's much closer to an "am" (the relationship) of existence.

I do not believe you can *find* love. You can find all kinds of relationships and people to have experiences with, but love is elusive and a mystery. It is a gift and a opportunity to come to a greater consciousness of life and yourself. Many times you will hear it said that a person's greatest work was done in a time of love. This is mostly because in love, the ego and the mind take a back seat to feelings. Love is not logical or reasonable, it simply ...*is*. It makes you feel complete and helps you to touch other parts of your life. It makes you feel more alive.

Love also reveals your pain and your issues. It uncovers the unconscious aspects that blind a person from fully experiencing life and gaining deeper awareness. Intimacy brings you close and, from within its comforting and safe cocoon, a haven whereby you can confront your deepest fears, doubts and hidden agendas together. As a result, these things are recognized, dealt with, and eventually cast off as so much excess baggage, allowing an even further growth in spiritual awareness and intimacy.

It is human nature to think we are grown, mature and loving; however, intimacy and caring often reveal that we are blind to aspects of our very nature that remain unrevealed to us. Love becomes a joyous partnership to explore together who we are, what we believe and where we are going. It can be a doorway to the very key to existence itself.

The Path of Love II

It seems that in life you search forever to find true love. I for one had many relationships, some were only sexual and others ran the gambit between friendship and hard knocks. One thing for sure, I did not know what I was looking for, but after each time I knew that it had to be fuller and more natural than what I had experienced in the last relationship. Sometimes I fell in a hole and let my darkest nature teach me lessons, hard lessons that came from a selfishness that is one-way and sought to steal and not share. So much of love's experiences are: what can you do for me -- and involves two people with one-sided views. No actual heart is there, and no conscious agreement to discover the unseen hold that you have on each other. Love is taken for granted and a missed opportunity to explore and uncover the depth of love thru a relationship.

Love is meant to be more than physical contact and emotional dependency. It is a door and a dance that can lead to deep realizations about life and afterlife. The key is to use unforeseen conflict as an opportunity to examine your feelings, thoughts and beliefs. Also to realize that reactions are a defense to prevent taking true responsibility for your actions. It is easier to blame another when you feel pain from a misunderstanding or perception, but far more honest to look within and say that I have an issue or problem that I need to address and look at. The fear that leads to fights is a missed opportunity to grow in love and awareness.

People know truth when they hear it, but will often make excuses for examining the roots of fear that lie beneath emotions that are raw and angry. We will do anything to protect our egos, avoid change and to take ultimate responsibility for our lives. For this reason we feel powerless to understand our connection to existence and our ability to control our destiny in the hands of a benevolent universe. We are not powerless, we are just protecting an illusion of self that is trying to prove it is real. There is no 'I' in love, but a sharing that leads to a greater realization of self on both persons' parts. Selfishness is always born of fear and greed soon follows.

You have enough, you are enough. This is the promise of love. A realization that you are not separate, but a part of everything seen and unseen. This door, this magic, this realization opens when we dare to share our deepest truth with another in honest exchanges. The longer that you defend your fear and ignorance, the longer and deeper the pain of separation. Love is a great humility and a great surrender, but not a taskmaster. It reveals the truth when we are ready to hear it.

My partner and friend, Catherine, placed on Facebook that you can't find love, and this is true. It is a gift that appears when you have tried every other thing and fallen so many times that you can't believe you still have hopes of it. But this is not the end. The real work begins because now you see that you have a precious diamond and you have to polish it and examine its facets. You have to keep it shining and glistening in the light. You must appreciate its beauty and also examine its flaws. It is not something you can ever take for granted. It is an opportunity to discover who you are, why you are, and where you are going.

The Magic of Courage in Intimacy

I have been thinking today about how courage comes into the equation of love and intimacy. So many things we hide from ourselves and our lovers. So many little foxes spoil the vine and hurt the growth of the orchard.

Recently in my relationship to Catherine, I felt the need to confess some of the dark secrets of my private life -- that psychological closet that we all have and hide and protect from everyone, except maybe a counselor or shrink. It was hard, it was scary, but it was one of those nagging things that comes up between lovers that you can't ignore or hide for long. You have to address it to continue along the journey of your love. You realize it could be a risk and you could ruin a good thing, but you hope that it might be a door to deeper love, forgiveness and compassion.

Love is not just a word. If it is, then you are not in *Love* and you do not understand its working in your life. It is a process of deeper awareness that can transcend the relationship and bring lovers in touch with their eternal halves, the unseen part of us that exists now beyond the veil of death.

So many people live with the idea of love, marriage and relationship in their minds that they never consider that it is a mystery, a discovery and a passage to deeper levels of intimacy and understanding. The universe gave us a gift of relationship so that we could journey through the mystery of this life together with someone and also share the mysteries of death together. This cannot happen unless we have the courage to be always honest, vulnerable and surrendered to each other deeply. This is NOT easy!

As we pass through the illusions of love to its deeper realities we die a thousand times to ideas we have cherished for years and considered to be true. Sometimes we find that we have nothing more to share and need to say goodbye. At other times we find a door to deeper realizations that can change the flavor of a relationship, but not its ingredients. Adjustments then have to be made and a choice of how to proceed.

Your love and mine is always at risk, a journey and a process of self discovery. If we choose to let it, it can strip us of pride, fear, insecurity, egotism and all the other vices that create a wall between our minds and our hearts. It is a far easier thing to share the journey of love with another person than to face the dark vaults of your unconscious alone. It is possible, but it is far too difficult when you are alone on this path we call life. Most of us need a mirror to see into and a companion to hold us when the night is long and you can't rest your mind. Every lover is a gift. Most of the time we all forget to open it and see what is inside. We appreciate how it looks and feels in our hands, and with our eyes, but we fail to examine it closer to see what treasures are hidden inside it.

If what you have is real love, it is very difficult to just walk away. No matter how painful or hurtful you might think your reality inside you is, we all have dark sides of incredibly complex feelings, thoughts and behaviors. You see we classify human as either good or bad, but those labels do not go far enough to define the complexity of humanness. We are all so afraid of ourselves that we had to create labels and images to accept ourselves, realizing we are more than the labels and restricting the possibility that we could and should discover more about the life that we are.

The world will never be happy until it discovers the ultimate truths or truth of existence. This I don't see happening anytime soon, but we will always rebel against the majority vote. Individualism is the nature of the universe and a gradual awakening to love, which is truth. Till then we will all have to make choices in our lives and relationships if we dare have the courage to reveal our uniqueness, our frailty and the unending depth of human experience and universal awareness we all have inside. You are never alone with the fears you carry inside you unless you choose not to share them with another who cares.

I am very fortunate to be in a loving relationship that took only 58 years to manifest and that we both have the understanding, maturity and love to face love's challenges together.

What is Love?

Good Question! People want it, need it, fear it and for sure they can't live a full life without it. But have you ever really asked yourself what love is or what it does for you? Some people say it makes you feel full or complete. You are able to feel life more deeply and passionately. You feel more connected to something beyond yourself. You are whole again. All of this is true, but these are *feelings* and they describe aspects of love's effect on you. They do not reveal what love actually is.

To describe love is to miss the boat on knowing love. The description is not the experience itself. It is far deeper and more alive than mere words can express. Words in fact can and do get in the way of love and life as anyone knows. To ask someone why they love you and then to hear a long dialogue about it is very disappointing. Love can't be described. It can only be felt. It is a <u>*knowing*</u> that words cant fulfill all by themselves.

To love yourself in this world is very rare and it's difficult. Two reasons are that you are separated from the womb of existence at birth and there is an angst about it we all carry inside. Secondly, we have thousands of people, institutions and groups telling us we are not good enough unless we meet their standards. We feel inferior most of our lives, until we find love, or it finds us.

Words cannot describe love or permit the feeling of love to fill us. It is beyond words and definitions. It is an awareness that we are more than we think we are, a remembrance from the very universe that something is missing and yet we can find it. A whisper of the unknown saying, "you don't know it all."

The best description I have of love is, an emptiness of yourself that is replaced by a fullness of yourself that words can't express adequately. It is a realization that you are not alone or separate, but a part of and connected to all of life in some way. It is the ultimate of feeling, minus the mind's need to describe, control, analyze or formulate..

About the Author

I was born Roman Catholic, became a fundamentalist minister at the age of 21, and then in 1983 I was introduced into Astrology. Since that time I have lived life as it has unfolded and discovered that each experience and event was a planned lesson or doorway into a deeper awareness or understanding of life. Trusting life and accepting the experiences that it brings you is the only real religion and offers us awareness when we do not shift the responsibility for our feelings onto others.

I offer astrology readings for those who are seeking insight into experiences that may be troubling their lives and my website, Magic Man's Universe is for anyone seeking deeper insight into Awareness and the unfolding of their life through experiences.

Magic Man's Universe
http://www.magicmansuniverse.com

www.ingramcontent.com/pod-product-compliance
Lightning Source LLC
Chambersburg PA
CBHW061251040426
42444CB00010B/2344